# LET'S GO TEAM:
## Cheer, Dance, March

# LET'S GO TEAM:
## Cheer, Dance, March

# Techniques of
# MARCHING BAND

## Judy Garty

**Mason Crest Publishers**
**Philadelphia**

Mason Crest Publishers, Inc.
370 Reed Road
Broomall, PA 19008
(866) MCP-BOOK (toll free)
www.masoncrest.com

2 3 4 5 6 7 8 9 10

Library of Congress Cataloging-in-Publication Data

Garty, Judy.
  Techniques of marching bands / Judy Garty.
    v. cm. — (Let's go team—cheer, dance, march)
Includes index.
Contents: The draw — The basics — The moves — The teamwork — The
flair — The rewards.
  ISBN 1-59084-539-0
 1. Marching bands—Juvenile literature. [1. Marching bands. 2. Bands
(Music)] I. Title. II. Series.
  MT733.4 .G372 2003
  784.8'3143—dc21

                                                                    2002015958

Produced by
Choptank Syndicate and Chestnut Productions
226 South Washington Street
Easton, Maryland  21601

Project Editors  Norman Macht and Mary Hull
Design  Lisa Hochstein
Picture Research  Mary Hull

Printed and bound in the Hashemite Kingdom of Jordan

## OPPOSITE TITLE PAGE

*Groups of musicians who play the same instrument march together as
a squad. Sometimes squads move in special
formations, such as circles or arcs, to create interesting
visual effects.*

# Table of Contents

# The Draw

**T**here's nothing like watching a parade filled with marching bands. Underneath your feet, the ground vibrates. You hear the next band coming. You stand on your tiptoes and stretch your neck to see what looks like a rolling sea of white feathers. Only two more floats to go before the pulse of the parade is in front of you. You start to march in place and clap your hands to the beat. The band's banner leads the way, followed by flag bearers who toss and wave colorful flags. The brass instruments sparkle in the sun, and all the musicians are in step with each other. Their music is happy and lively. It makes you think of the circus, of ice cream cones, and of fireworks.

*For people who love music, the lure of a marching band is hard to resist. The powerful music, colorful costumes, and synchronized steps of a marching band stir the hearts of both spectators and participants.*

*Marching band members usually perform in a special dress uniform with decorative pants, jackets, and gloves. Military bandsmen traditionally wore decorative braid on their uniforms, and many school bands continue that practice today.*

Drums boom. Petite piccolos look almost like toys, and they play bird-like, very high notes. Tubas deliver a deep um-pah, um-pah, um-pah. Cymbals clang with a bang. Sleek trombones slide in and out. Rows of flutes and saxophones and trumpets send their notes soaring. Everyone watching starts to clap, and a lot of people are waving small flags they brought with them.

Playing in a marching band is for anyone who likes music and marching. Most young people who belong to marching bands participate through their schools or after-school organizations and clubs. Music and marching have gone together since ancient times. In the United States, high school and college bands began to grow in the 1920s, when they started performing at football games. Even though girls participated in high school music programs and a few college marching bands from the late 1890s, they weren't fully accepted as members of college marching bands until the 1970s. Today, the marching band doors are wide open to all young people. It is common for marching bands to have 100 or more members.

"A lot of kids can find their home in the marching band," says Alan Rick Temby of Indiana, who writes marching band drills for high schools and colleges in six states. Temby, who has been writing shows for 24 years, says he has seen band members who are blind, one-armed, or in wheelchairs pushed by other band members. The 1940 University of Wisconsin Badger Band had a blind trombone player who marched in the band with the help of band members on each side of him giving directions. Band members have to work together as a team.

If you are interested in a marching band you have to decide what you want to do when you march. Many marchers play musical instruments. The instruments in a marching band are ones you can carry while you walk. You couldn't play a piano in a marching band, but piano lessons might make learning to play other instruments easier for you. You can start learning to play a musical instrument at just about any age. Music lessons will help you learn to play an instrument like a trumpet or a flute. Many students rent instruments before buying them. Usually students try out their instruments by renting them to be sure they like the instrument and want to continue learning to play it. If the instruments are too big to carry home, like tubas and drums, then students might have to play their instruments in school.

Music teachers, representatives from music stores, and other instructors will help you decide what instruments may fit you. Many elementary schools offer music lessons. If you start learning to play a marching band instrument in grade school, you can continue your lessons in middle and high school. You can even take lessons during the summer months from a private teacher or by attending some kind of music camp or drum corps (a drum corps is a kind of marching band). Sometimes young people learn to play one instrument when they are young and then switch to a different instrument when they are older. Some middle schools have marching bands; some don't. Marching bands are very common at the high school and university levels.

There are other people besides musicians in marching bands. Marching bands often have baton twirlers or a color guard who carry flags or rifles. Even if you do not have a marching band at your middle school, you will probably be able to find one at your high school or nearby. Most marching bands have classes or camps to teach you what you need to know. Bands for beginners can help you learn the basics.

**TYPES OF MARCHING BANDS**

There are many kinds of marching bands: drum corps, traditional marching bands, show bands, pipe bands, comedy bands, circus bands, scout bands, and scramble bands. Traditional bands, drum corps, pipe bands, and scout bands are the most common marching bands for young people. Beginning marching band members are usually middle school age, but there can be flag bearers, baton twirlers, and drum corps and community band members who are younger. For example, Sergeant Chris Reesor, bass drum instructor and drum major for the 48th Highlanders of Canada, started studying drums at age four. He marched with the 9th Toronto Boys' Brigade Band when he was seven.

Drum and bugle corps groups are most often known simply as drum corps. They use brass and percussion instruments, and they learn routines for competitions. Drum Corps International (DCI), an organization that sponsors performances and competitions around the

## A DRUM CORP THAT MIXES AGES AND BEATS

The Rhythm Regiment Drum and Bugle Corps is a percussion ensemble from the Long Beach area of California. Its members are as young as two years old and as old as 13. Their multi-cultural music is a blend of Afro-Cuban, Caribbean, Native American, Asian, South Pacific, and urban hip-hop beats.

world, has three divisions. Each division has a set number of corps members and different distances they are allowed to travel. The smallest corps is Division III with up to 60 members. Like the 61- to 128-member corps groups of Division II, they stay pretty close to home and often compete on weekends. Division I groups have distinguished themselves in competition and have won the honor of making national tours. Many towns, cities, and communities have their own drum corps groups who perform and compete locally.

Traditional marching bands are found in schools and communities. They can be performing bands, competing bands, or both. Many traditional marching bands march in local parades, give local concerts, and travel to places like Disneyland. Traditional marching band training usually begins in middle school where students learn to play their instruments in a concert band program.

Pipe and drum bands can be found from Scotland to Hawaii. These bands usually wear tartan plaids. The Pipes and Drums of the Atlantic Watch of New Jersey has over 100 performers from age 7 to 70 and has performed in Scotland for crowds of over 300,000 spectators.

The Bournemouth Carnival Band is a comedy marching band from England. The musicians are age 16 and up, and they play brass, bell-lyres (the marching version of glockenspiels, shaped liked lyres), bugles, and drums. In the past the band has worn Batman, cowboy and Indian, Santa Claus, snowmen, and Spiderman costumes. This charity group helps raise money for children's causes, and it uses props and fake explosions to entertain crowds.

Peru, Indiana has the Peru Circus Band that performs at each of the 11 circus shows when the circus comes to town. The band has 130 members, some of whom used to play in the local high school band. Almost everyone else in the show is from the community, so the entire show has a community flavor.

A handful of colleges have scramble bands. A scramble band performs during the halftime of a football game. The scramble band show is funny and full of jokes and skits. They move on the field without the usually organized patterns. Some of the musicians play unusual instruments like mailboxes, mannequins, slide whistles, violins, or weed wackers. Others in the band might dance or juggle.

Different cities and neighborhoods have special kinds of marching bands. In the United Kingdom, there are over 100 Scout bands. One of the top honors for a Scout band is to be chosen to lead the St. George's Day Parade at Windsor Castle.

Brass bands have cornets or trumpets, euphoniums (brass instruments resembling tubas), French horns or tenor horns, trombones, tubas, and percussion instruments like timpani, battery, mallet, keyboard, and electric bass. The Triangle Youth Brass Band of the Research Triangle Park area in North Carolina was the 2002 National American Brass Band Association Champion in the youth division.

Bands, such as those representing the Salvation Army, Hallmark greeting card company, or the United States Automobile Association insurance company, tend to be adult bands.

Northern Lights Home School Marching Band is a summer activity for home schooled students in West Michigan. This independent group marched in the 2000 National Independence Day parade in Washington, D.C.

Some bands have a unique style. The Cal Band of the University of California at Berkeley, California, is a high-stepping show band. Marchers lift their knees really high and almost jump with each step while they are marching. That kind of marching gives the band a workout. Besides the regular Cal Band, this university has a Straw Hat Band. Brown University Band may be the world's only ice skating band. The Mounted Band entertains on horseback in Milwaukee, Wisconsin's annual circus parade.

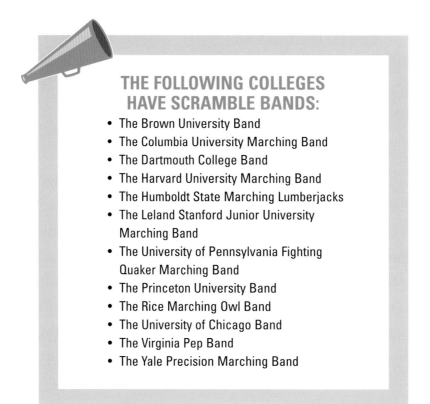

### THE FOLLOWING COLLEGES HAVE SCRAMBLE BANDS:

- The Brown University Band
- The Columbia University Marching Band
- The Dartmouth College Band
- The Harvard University Marching Band
- The Humboldt State Marching Lumberjacks
- The Leland Stanford Junior University Marching Band
- The University of Pennsylvania Fighting Quaker Marching Band
- The Princeton University Band
- The Rice Marching Owl Band
- The University of Chicago Band
- The Virginia Pep Band
- The Yale Precision Marching Band

*Many marching bands and drum corps have a color guard. Guard members add to the performance by twirling flags or rifles in time to the music.*

Marching bands play fast songs, slow songs, patriotic music, jazz, and whatever else fits their show. Marching bands move, so the marchers have to learn drills. Practicing routines lets marchers know how big a step they should take, how they should move about the field or in the street, where they should be for playing different parts of the music, and how they should look when they're together.

*Show bands, like the Cal Band at the University of California at Berkeley, use a high-stepping march style.*

Marching band shows almost always happen outdoors. If the marching band is performing in a parade, the audience can see and hear them only when they are close by. If the marching band gives a field show, the audience is seated and can see and hear the whole show.

Marching band is a group activity. If you join a marching band, you have to learn your part well so you can help make the group look and sound good. You will need to go to every scheduled band lesson and rehearsal. You will have to take care of any uniform or equipment the band director gives you, and follow the band leader's directions.

Marching bands perform for other people. Your band might march in a holiday parade, or compete with other bands for trophies or recognition. If your band is mostly a parade band, you can expect to practice both indoors and outdoors. If your band goes to competitions during the band season, you will be taught routines to perform on your football field. If you belong to a drum corps, you can expect to be on the road for two summer months.

David Kliss, co-director of the Kennedy Middle School Marching Band in Germantown, Wisconsin, has been working with youth marching bands for 29 years. His current parade band has 200 members who perform in the spring and summer of their sixth and seventh grade years. The band spends the month of March learning the music, April memorizing the music, and May practicing marching. According to Kliss, growth spurts, different heights and paces, and instruments designed for high school students can make the physical coordination a challenge. Kliss says, "It's really okay if things aren't perfect; it's a learning experience. It gets them out into the community. It gets them learning about marching. It's the largest audience they can perform for. They love it; the enthusiasm is very high."

# The Basics

After you know what kind of marching bands are near you and which kind you like best, you can find out how to become a band member. Once you are a member, you will practice almost every day. Even when you are not practicing, there are things you should know about keeping yourself healthy and ready for marching. Your band director will set goals for you to help you progress through the band program.

Joining a band happens in several ways. At many schools and clubs, people audition, or try out, for the band. At an audition, you are usually asked to play a couple songs on your instrument, or demonstrate your talent

*Marching band requires a lot of time and devotion. In addition to practices during the school year, band members are encouraged to attend summer band camps where they may spend up to twelve hours a day perfecting their routines.*

before the band director and others in charge of the band. If a band needs ten new flute players and twenty audition, then only half of them will get to be in the band. Sometimes a club will have three or four bands, and your audition will decide which band you are ready for. In that situation, everyone who auditions will get to join the band. For many school bands and drum corps, auditions are held in the fall to decide which players are good enough to be in solos.

Drum corps and community band members often pay fees to help pay for things like uniforms, music teachers, the use of the place where practice is held, and signing up for competitions. Most marching band members help raise funds for travel expenses and operating costs. There are expenses in marching band participation. The cost of buying an instrument, if that is required, and paying membership dues can be hundreds of dollars. Sometimes scholarships are available.

## FLORIDA AND SCOTLAND BOUND BY BAGPIPES

Dunedin, Florida and Stirling, Scotland are sister cities. Both share a Highlander Band heritage. In 1957, the Dunedin Junior High School Band became a Highlander Band. It performs at the opening spring training home game of the Toronto Blue Jays. The middle school has five other bands, including the Grade V Pipe Band that competes against high school, college, and adult bands. The City of Dunedin also has a pipe band.

*Marching bands are organized into squads of musicians who play the same instrument. Squads learn to move and turn together as a group.*

Depending on where you live and what program you are in, the regular marching band season may be short. In some places, the marching band or drum corps season is only as long as the summer. For most high schools and colleges, the season is fall and spring. During the season, you might have band every day in school or a couple times a week in your community. Whatever the marching band season is, there are ways to get yourself ready before the season starts. Many programs depend on band camps to prepare their marchers. At high school, for instance, students may be required to spend a week in August at school. Often the days are hot and filled with hard work. Marchers may be "working" for eight or even

12 hours a day during band camp. Drum corps practice days can run 10 to 12 hours long.

Preseason is the first time the band gets the music for the season and begins to learn the drills. Since marching bands may begin to compete in the fall, the band has to learn its routines quickly. Band camp work is often a combination of field marching, sectional rehearsals, and large group instruction with the band director. One important thing the members learn is how to pace. The marching band step or cadence needs to be uniform—the same amount of space for every person for each step. Quite often that step is measured at 22.5 inches on the field and 30 inches in a parade. That sameness helps the routines and the marching look polished. Your band director will tell you the size of each step and how many steps fill five yards. Some bands march with eight steps per five yards, and some march six steps per five yards. It doesn't matter if you are tall or short; practice gives the whole band time to make adjustments so they can move together well.

Most marching band music is written in 2/4 time with eight counts in four measure phrases. Four measure phrases are four bars of music that express one idea, much as four sentences might combine to form a paragraph. Learning about such phrasing is one way to become a master marching band member. Using the eight to five pace works out to one phrase per yard line. With practice, you learn how fast or slow to move on the field, how to keep in line with the rest of the band, and how to move into different formations while playing on the field.

Practice means repeating something over and over to make it as good as you possibly can. In the same way that athletes prepare to run, musicians get ready to march and perform by doing warm-ups. Patrick Dunnigan, Director of the Marching Chiefs at Florida State University, says that the best marching bands never skip their warm-ups. Dunnigan says 10 to 15 minute warm-ups are a good way to listen to each other, even if it's windy, and routine warm-ups help each member of the band get better at what they do. Marching bands warm up so when they march together, all the details of their routines are in order: how they hold their instruments, how much air they use to play their instruments, how they coordinate air flow with their tongues, and how they match the music to their marching steps.

Keeping up with marching band means paying attention to many things. Besides regular music lessons where you learn how to play your instrument better, you will need to learn to play different scales, listen to harmonies, and train your ear to understand why certain notes sound good together. The more you learn, the better you will be able to perform in your band.

The same is true for the band's non-musicians. The color guard and drum majors benefit from practice the same as those who play instruments. Practicing together makes the routines easier so when the band performs, all the marching band members know exactly what to do.

No matter how much you learn about music and marching, there will be surprise lessons along the way. You might have to cope with a judge's decision that was not what you hoped it would be, or you might have to change your performing plans because of the weather. Continuous practice will help you be able to handle those lessons well.

Mike Lekrone, director of the high-stepping University of Wisconsin Band, says marching band members have to be tough enough to "eat a rock!" Marching band activity gives a workout to many parts of your body. Musicians march while holding and playing their instruments, which can be heavy or awkward to carry for miles in a parade. Making sure each body part is working as it should is important. Proper shoes are essential.

**STYLES OF MARCHING**

There are different ways to march: traditional military style, drum corps style, and the high-stepping show band style. Traditional style is like military marching. More and more traditional bands are adopting the corps style, but only a small number of Big Ten colleges use the high step style. Whichever way your band marches will involve very specific motions from your ankles, feet, hips, and knees. When you march correctly, the upper body will not move up and down at all. When you have practiced marching quite a while, the marching step will be natural to you. You will march just like everyone else in the band without thinking about it.

One corps style of marching that uses the eight-to-five pace starts with the foot flat on the ground. When marching begins, the heel comes up and the ankle bends down. Keeping the foot pointed down, the toe touches the

*Hand-eye coordination is an essential skill for color guard members, who perform a variety of complex motions.*

ground first. The knee lifts medium high to make a right angle, and the hip acts like a hinge that lets the rest of the leg move forward. Marching correctly also affects how you play your instrument. If you are moving too much, you might miss notes. Marching on the balls of your feet, for instance, helps prevent brass players from banging their instruments into their lips.

Another corps technique is the roll step. Using this gentler step, one heel leaves the ground and in the next step comes down first. The stride is even and low like a roll, with the knee moving the same way it does in a regular walking step. The heel points toward the ground before it touches down, and the bottom of your shoe will be visible to anyone watching you from the front.

People who are just learning to march make common mistakes such as walking like a duck, bending forward at the waist, and shuffling. Your heels and toes should not be hitting the ground at the same time. Sometimes band directors give marchers exercises with silly names like "toothpaste squeeze" and "bug crunch" to focus their attention on certain parts of the moves. Marchers need to keep their heads up and faces forward.

Other members of the marching band must also pay attention to detail. Members of the color guard must have

## A CANADIAN MARCHING BAND WITH A CIVIC HEART

The 562 Cabot Squadron Band is a 40-piece marching band from North Sydney, Nova Scotia, Canada. Its members are age 13 to 18, and they play glockenspiels, drums, and trumpets. They lead the local parade on Decoration Sunday or Remembrance Day, and they march in events like the Quebec Winter Carnival Parade, the Bangor, Maine, Santa Claus Parade, and the Annapolis Valley Apple Blossom Parade. They also perform concerts at senior citizen homes and hospitals.

strong arms and good hand-eye coordination to hold and move their flags or rifles. Baton twirlers have to catch the batons they throw into the air.

Being in a marching band requires many skills. Band directors are responsible for teaching them. Listening to the director's instruction and asking questions when you are not sure about how to do something are good ways to learn. Band directors, drum majors, and color guard captains are constantly evaluating the band's form and sound and will offer suggestions as needed. Most marching bands are a mixture of ages. Often an experienced band member marches beside a beginner and offers a model to follow.

Band directors set goals for their marchers. They listen for good tone and intonation—good musical sound with the accurate highness or lowness known as pitch. Each instrument requires different skills. Wind instrument players, for instance, must learn proper tonguing attack and be able to correctly finger different scales and arpeggios, the notes of a chord. Percussionists have to be able to read the four rhythmic categories: common time, alla breve, 6/8 time, and compound time. Your musical goals will include understanding musical terms, the signs for lengths of notes, and the dynamics, or volume of sound, produced by an instrument. The longer you are a musician, the more challenging you can expect the music to be.

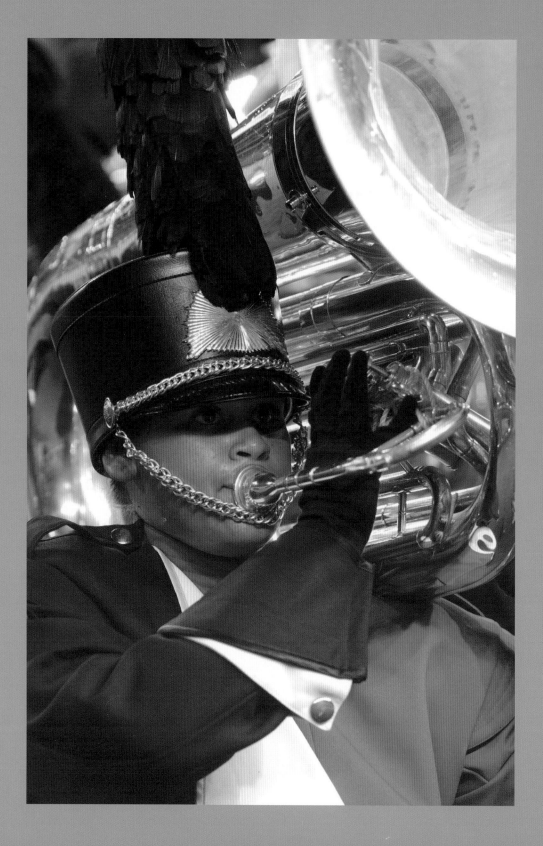

# The Moves

Even though marching bands develop their own style and personality, they have many of the same voice, written, or whistle commands. Band members work hard to match their marching steps to give the band a uniform movement. Marchers who use a medium high knee lift can get 120 beats per minute in their cadence.

Traditional marching bands that perform on football fields start with a block formation. Each performer is assigned a number. For example, the first row of instruments—perhaps trumpets—might be named A1, A2, A3, A4, A5, and A6. The second row would be B1, B2, B3, B4, B5, and B6. Each person is given a set of charts that

*It takes a lot of practice to learn to play music well while marching. Some of the larger instruments, like the tuba, pose an extra challenge.*

uses those letters and numbers to tell them where to stand for each formation. Band members can move from one formation to another by a follow-the-leader method or by disbursement. When the band disburses, it leaves one set of positions and moves randomly into the next position without following a leader. Marching bands that use a drum corps style chart their maneuvers for four-person squads rather than individuals. Marchers move from one formation to another by drum cadence or music.

On the field or in a parade, the band director or drum major uses voice commands to give the band directions. The way each band gives commands may differ slightly, but many commands come in two parts. The first word tells who the command is for or which direction is important. The second part tells the band when to start. The voice commands are given in rhythm, and some syllables are accented to make them clearer to understand.

**Fall in!** is the command for everyone to line up in their places.

**Detail at the ready** calls for feet apart, head down, and left hand over the right. On the fourth count, the

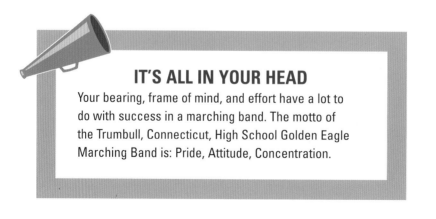

## IT'S ALL IN YOUR HEAD
Your bearing, frame of mind, and effort have a lot to do with success in a marching band. The motto of the Trumbull, Connecticut, High School Golden Eagle Marching Band is: Pride, Attitude, Concentration.

marcher snaps into position—one, two, three, hut—by bringing the left foot in and the hands up.

**Band, ten-hut!** or **detail ha-ten-hut!** calls the band to attention. Each band member should be facing forward with eyes looking straight ahead with pride, chin up, shoulders back, elbows frozen, stomach in, legs straight, heels together, toes at a 30- to 45-degree angle, and back arched slightly backward. Musicians should hold their instruments in one hand, not both. Marchers should check their rank, file, and diagonal and make sure they are in line. Marchers have to be careful not to lock their knees. That posture can lead to fainting or heat exhaustion. The band director will tell you if you are supposed to line up with your toes or your heels on the yard lines.

**Band, rest!** gives the band a break. When this command is given, the band members can relax. They have to stay in the general area, but they can talk to each other, sit down if seats are available, or remove their hats. Some bands require members to stand at the band, rest. This command would be used if the band has to wait quite a while before it performs.

**Band, at ease!** is another relaxing break, but the band members cannot move the right foot. Some bands allow quiet talk, others do not. Many times this command is given when the band director has to make an announcement or explain something to the band.

**Parade, rest!** means some relaxing but no talking or moving. In this position, the right foot remains planted and the left foot moves 12 to 15 inches left. Some bands keep the left foot on the ground and on beat four move the right foot sideways to shoulder width. Other bands have the hands crossed on forearms left over right in fists against the biceps. Both feet should be pointed forward. Often the left hand is placed behind the back at the waist, with the palm facing out. The marcher remains facing forward and looking straight ahead. Some bands answer "hite" or "hut" when they slide their left feet into parade, rest position. This shout is called on the up beat of the second count. You can only do the parade, rest move from an attention position. After parade, rest you can do ten-hut, at ease, or dismissed.

**Band, ha-bout face!** is used to turn the band around. About face is the actual command, but "ha-bout face" is how the command is pronounced. It is given from an attention position and is the same as the marching command rear march or to the rear. The four-count move begins on the first beat of the second set of four beats. It requires three movements: standing on the balls of both feet and taking a right step forward; turning 180 degrees; placing the right foot smartly next to the left with even weight. The three movements are counts with a quick rhythm of eighth notes. Sometimes the band will count out loud—one, two, three—for each step. About face moves add color to a performance. There are variations of about face that add a hop or a kick for a more military or show look.

**Left, face!** is a standard two-count military move that turns the band a right angle to the left. Some bands use three counts for this move. It is given from an attention stance and is the same as left flank when the band is

*Marching band members have charts that tell them where to stand during each formation. By following commands, they make sure they start, stop, and change direction at exactly the same time.*

marching. You lift the left toe and the right heel and pivot. Turn and together, one-two. The first part is like the about face. Both feet carry the weight of the body and the right foot steps forward. You push on the ball of the right foot to turn the body 90 degrees left. The right foot then joins the left in standing.

**Right, face!** turns the band 90 degrees to the right. This command is the same as the marching command of right flank. The three counts are the same as left, face, except the turn is to the right. You lift the right toe and left heel and make a quarter turn. In a flank type movement, the right foot never leaves the ground. It just pivots. In a kick style movement, the counts are more accented.

Some marching movements are given to band members as directions on their drill sheets. Any of the following moves, marked with initials, could be written into a drill. These movements can also be given as oral commands during a rehearsal.

**Halt (H)** is a stop command that separates mark time, or marching in place, from stride step, which is forward march. Though the halt can happen on either foot, usually the band will stop its forward motion on the left foot and bring the right foot up and even next to the left foot on count two. The last note of count two in a march might be a stinger or a silent beat. A stinger is a sustained note that starts with a hard attack, backs off, and then crescendos. Some bands exaggerate the halt step by locking the right knee or leaning forward slightly before stepping off. Bands that bring the right foot down on "one" and the left foot down on "two" use a small kick as the heels meet and shout "One, two!" after a halt.

**Kick halt** or **snap halt (KH or SH)** gives the stop some pizzaz. In the kick halt, the right foot swings in an arc to the right before it lands next to the left foot. In the snap halt, the right foot is raised higher than normal and then snaps down beside the left foot.

**Mark time (MT)** means marching in place. It is used often and takes a lot of practice to do correctly. There are several styles of mark time. Different bands focus on lifting the heels, popping the knees, tapping the foot, or rolling the foot. Some bands use four bass drum beats for mark time. The most important thing in mark time is that everyone in the band is doing it the same way.

**Forward march (FM)** means to move forward. Sometimes the body is bent back slightly at the waist to give the move a dignified look. When the posture is right, marchers often stand taller than they normally do. It is almost like you are gliding along the ground and have grown an extra inch. The arched back helps avoid problems like leaning forward or stepping off on the wrong foot. The movement has the feet rolling heel to ball, and it gives a smooth look. There is no moving from the waist up, and the knees move only slightly. Marchers cover eight steps in five yards with a 22.5-inch step. Yard lines on the football field help marchers space out their steps, but bands have to be able to march without yard lines, too.

**Rear march** and **to the rear (RM** or **TTR)** are the same command. It is like about face, but it happens when the marcher is in motion. It starts with a normal stride forward. The left foot should not leave the ground when executing this movement. The left foot stops the forward motion and you turn around 180 degrees to the left on the ball of the right foot. Balance is important to do this step well.

**Left flank (LF)** is a turn to the left. The right foot remains stationary so the body can pivot on the balls of both feet a quarter turn to the left and continue marching.

**Right flank (RF)** sounds like it should be the same as a left flank only turning right instead of left. There are actually four versions of a right flank move. In the correct right flank, the left foot stops the forward body motion and the marcher turns to the right. Right flank moves cannot happen at the same time as left flank moves. If you are taught the incorrect right flank, the right foot stays on the ground but the body slows down instead of stopping. This doesn't mean the directions are not right; it is just another name for this variation. Just like making a right turn on a bicycle, the body will lean a little. This move has the same rhythm as the left flank, and it allows movements from both flanks at the same time. This move is harder than the other right flank moves, but it allows left

## FUNDRAISING IDEAS FOR YOUR BAND

Some band boosters have invented ways of earning money beyond traditional candy, pizza, and plant sales. The Blue Raider Band of Texas offers "No Cooking Nights" through seven area restaurants that give dining discounts to benefit the band. The Elko, Nevada High School band holds a steak and hamburger dinner fundraiser. In Marietta, Georgia, band members recycle newspapers, earn $10 in band credit by working a three-hour shift at the VFW bingo hall, or earn a $15 band credit by working sporting events at the Georgia Dome. Donors in Onalaska, Wisconsin, who give $1,000 or more are recognized with a city flower garden that is tended over the summer by volunteer band members. For a $20 donation, Onalaska band members will serenade a Valentine sweetie of your choice with three songs and a carnation.

and right flanks to happen at the same time. The fancy right flank or special right flank starts on the right foot. The left foot spins to the left and the body turns three-quarters of a circle in the left direction. The whole near-circle move has to be done in one step. It takes practice to do this spinning move accurately.

**Left oblique (LO)** is very much like the left flank, except that the turn in this move is less than 90 degrees—very often 45 degrees to the left. After this move, the marchers will be lined up diagonally.

**Right oblique (RO),** like right flank moves, turns the marcher to the right. The right oblique turn, though, is less than 90 degrees—usually a 45 degree right turn.

**Open front (OF)** can be a diagonal or a flank move. In a diagonal move, the marchers make oblique moves. Some marchers near the center just keep marching ahead but with shorter steps. In a flank move, the center marchers mark time while marchers to their left and right flank in groups and then flank back to the front.

**Close front (CF)** is the opposite of open front. It, too, can be made diagonally or as a flank movement.

A marching band looks better when everyone stands the same whether they are in motion or not, so knowing exactly how to stand and move are important details. You will be taught how high to lift your knee when you march. Only the show bands lift the knee higher than a walking or marching pace. A straight back and shoulders that go back will give you good posture. Usually you do not have to swing your instrument, but your band director will let you know if you do. You might have to swing your arm,

*Good posture is essential for marching band members. These musicians are bent backward slightly at the waist so that they appear to be almost gliding along.*

though, slightly away from your body. British style bands exaggerate the arm swing, and high-stepping bands bend the elbow.

Starting off on the correct foot leaves a good impression. Sometimes bands practice a first pace by kicking out the left foot about six inches from the ground and landing on the ground on the count of one. Bands may also add fancy movements, called special licks, to give their marching a polished look. A band might fake a pivot by making it look like it is going to go in one direction but then turning in the opposite direction. A freeze could be a surprise move to keep the audience interested in what the band is doing. Saluting with hats or taking a bow are other special moves. Once in a while a band will include dance steps in their program or complete circle turns called whirls. There is also a step that looks like a walking goose and an off-beat goose step where the foot is up on the beat and down on the second beat. Other special movements include different ways of bringing the instruments into playing position. In a drum corps show, different sets of musicians and guards may be performing different moves at the same time.

When any part of learning music or marching is tricky it is called a tough lick. For instance, it might take you a long time to master the rhythm of a piece, or you might find a couple bars of music difficult to play. You might not be sure how to purse your lips or how to angle your instrument to hit a certain note. You might find some notes too fast, too high, or too low to play correctly easily. However difficult the music might be for you, your band director will have advice about how to master even the toughest licks.

# The Teamwork

**T**eamwork is what makes a marching band successful. Besides all the individual things you have to learn to do, all the marchers in a band have to perform as a unit. Different drills require different teams of marchers to move different ways on the field. Much of the rehearsal time is spent working together to make the routines come to life.

Most bands are organized into squads that move and turn as a group. Squads are groups of musicians who play the same instrument. A squad could consist of four members who stand two steps or 45 inches apart. Each squad is given a number. The numbers are written on drill sheets

*Marching band members must move their ankles, feet, hips, and knees in precise ways in order to stay in step and look polished.*

*In order for people in the stands to see a formation like this one in the shape of a wedge, all the band members must be moving with precision.*

so each squad will know where they need to be for different parts of a routine. Squad members can stand in close interval—close together with elbows touching—or more spaced apart in an open interval—about an arm's length away from one another.

Squads move in many ways, especially when performing in a show. Parts of the band may be moving in arcs or circles while other parts are dancing, running across the field, or forming a block with a section of the band. The pictures the band or corps makes on the field should fit with the theme and music it has chosen. Squad movements will jazz up the show, adding the burst of an arc, crisscrossing lines, or artistic dancing to the performance.

Dress movements include dress right, dress left, and dress center. There are close interval and open interval dress movements, too. The term dress describes interval and alignment—how the band members are spaced and lined up. In any part of a maneuver, dress is a detail the band has to perfect. Dressing movements help the band arrange the position of the members before a show maneuver. All dress movements occur in one count, and dress position is held until the command is given to move. Sometimes bands and corps use an interval stick to check the line. The center of each 22.5-inch space should line up with the center of each band member in the line.

Close interval dress position is the same as for attention, except the squad members snap their heads to the right or left to look down the line and correct any part of the line that needs it. For a dress center move, the center band member stays at attention while the others dress, or

## PHYSICAL FITNESS WORKOUT

The Yorkton Regional High Marching 100 Raiders of Yorkton, Saskatchewan, had two years to prepare to represent Canada at the 1998 Tournament of Roses Parade on New Year's Day in Pasadena, California. Their motto became "The journey is just as important as the destination." The 206-member band marched for miles in their community and worked with an aerobics instructor to prepare for their 5.5-mile parade route with its 2-mile march to the starting line. Besides the one million spectators, the parade had 450 million television viewers worldwide.

*An alignment in which band members stand elbow to elbow is called an open interval.*

line up, using the center as a guide. Similar movements happen with dress right and left. For open interval dress movements, band members extend an arm in the direction they are dressing to or lining up to.

Squad turns can change the marching direction up to a full circle of 360 degrees. There are center pivot turns which move a quarter turn quickly in two counts, and end pivot turns that require four counts. The center pivot can change a squad's position on the field by 2.5 yards.

Column movements are ways of moving a line of marchers. These movements include the gate or end pivot turn, the open interval four man 90 degree turn, the oblique turn, the minstrel turn, and the square turn. All of these moves require each person in the squad to move differently, so practice is a must. If the line is too crowded it will sag, and if it is too loose it may fan out incorrectly.

Step drills are an effective way to add variety and symmetry to a performance. There are different step drills: step-one, step-two, step-four, step-eight, and step-sixteen are the most common. The step drill can start from one or several points in the line. In a step-four drill, four marchers take a sideways step together. They halt step just before they step off. Step drills can start from a line, a curved arc, a file, or other positions.

Formations are a huge part of a marching band show. When a marching band or drum corps is on a field or performing in a competition, it wants to give the audience something to look at and enjoy. At a football game, a college band might form the letters of their school or the score of the game. In a competition, a marching band might move into the shape of an animal, create geometric designs, or move in and out of designs that look like pictures. It takes time to learn the formations and to time your steps to the right places in the music.

# The Flair

**I**f you've ever seen a movie in which soldiers are marching to a chant of "Left . . . left . . . left, right, left," then you know how a traditional parade band moves. But as you have already read, there are many more moves that go into a marching band performance. Often, the parade band will stop along the parade route and give a show that involves movement other than marching.

The color guard of a marching band can add flair and drama to the performance. Guard members strive to be creative and inventive with their props in a way that suits the music that is being played. Even though all marching band members work as a team, the color guard has its

*Guard members, performing at a Drum Corps International event, use their bodies, expressions, and equipment to create an athletic art form that complements the music.*

own set of maneuvers. Drum corps and pipe bands also have movements that are slightly different from those of other bands.

## COLOR GUARD

Color guard is a mix of costume, props, dance, and drill. Color guard members carry flags and sometimes rifles. When the guard in a drum corps performs, each member carries several props onto the field. Flags are generally five feet high, and rifles are about three feet long. The rifles are props only, not working guns. The flag and rifle guard can perform together, separately, or one at a time. Just as musicians have maneuvers, the color guard has to learn flag and rifle techniques and choreography. Color guard members have to march and follow commands like the rest of the band, and they also have to handle their flags or rifles with control in a way that adds flash to the show. Color guards have to practice often and work carefully to avoid injuries.

There are some basic commands and spins as well as room for creativity. It is not uncommon for one song to have 30 or more moves. The moves for the flag bearers are the same as for the rifle bearers but can look different because of the props. Color guard often invent their own moves or name moves according to how they look: back scratch, butterfly, cradle, dolphin, lasso, hammer, helicopter, hourglass, rainbow, or windshield wiper. Color guard members cannot turn their heads unless it is part of a routine. To keep their concentration, they cannot smile unless directed to do so.

*Color guard performers combine running and dancing with the use of equipment such as flags, rifles, or sabers.*

Here are some of the basic color guard commands:

**Attention** is a command in which the feet are ducked: the ankles are together and the toes are pointed 45 degrees outward. The chin is up, and you hold the flag in front of you at the right side, in front of the right foot. The right arm is at the tab, or at the bottom of the silk, or flag. The left arm is at the top of the silk and makes a backwards "L" from the shoulder to the flag in front of the face. Your eyes peek over the left arm.

*Carrying flags with the marching band's colors, this color guard is in constant motion as it performs in the 2001 Rose Parade.*

**Right shoulder** is a command that can follow attention. Your left hand is placed over the bottom stopper, and your right hand holds the flag at the tab. Your left hand should be right in front of your belt buckle or belly button, and the flag should be in the center of your body hanging straight up and down. **Left shoulder** is a reverse of right shoulder.

**Present arms** has the flag angled at 45 degrees in front of your face. The left arm is bent waist high, and the right arm is straight out holding the flag at the tab.

**Order arms** is a command that returns the flag to a right shoulder position.

**Forward march** has the guard cradle the flag at the right elbow. The right hand is at the bottom of the silk and the left arm makes a fist on the hip. When marching begins, the left foot steps forward and both hands move slightly left and back with a snap.

**Parade rest** has the feet apart in line with the shoulders. The flag is close to your body and at 45 degrees from the center of the body. The flag is on the left side, and the pole is diagonally in front of your chest. The left hand grips the top of the flag with the left elbow straight out. The right hand is at the tab.

**Right slam** starts with a right shoulder. Next you bring the flag down at a 45 degree angle, pointing it to the ground. The flag will be across your body in a diagonal line. Your left hand will be in front of your left shoulder and cover the top of the pole. Your right hand should be slightly out from your hip, and your palm will face upward. **Left slam** is the same as the right slam except you switch your hands.

**Front present** starts with a right shoulder. Then you push your right arm completely straight forward and parallel to the ground. Your left hand stays at your belly button.

**Left present** has the top hand moving left until your elbow is in front of your chin.

**Right present** tries to keep the flag in front of the right shoulder.

**Flat** starts at right shoulder and you bring the flag down until both arms are loose and straight down. The center of your pole should line up with the center of your body.

**Drop spin** starts at the right shoulder with a counter-clockwise flag spin. Let your left hand hang at your side, and move the flag until it is completely upside down. Your right hand will also come down and in front. Put your left palm down in front of you, turn your hand 90 degrees clockwise so your thumb points to the ground. Keeping the palm of your hand facing the left and your thumb down, grasp the pole below your right hand. Both thumbs will point away from you, and you can take your right

## PIPE BANDS

Beginners in pipe bands start on a recorder-like instrument called a practice chanter. After they know how to finger, they begin to learn the bagpipe. It is easier to learn this instrument if you start young. Middle school students can become good bagpipe players in less than two years. But the cost of bagpipes can be prohibitive. When the Lord Selkirk Boy Scout Pipe Band began in 1957 in Winnipeg, Manitoba, Canada, bagpipes cost $85 apiece. Today, the cost ranges from $850 to $2500 but averages $1,400 each.

hand off and let it hang at your side. Keep moving the flag counterclockwise until it turns right side up, then grasp it again with your right under your left. All of these moves require a lot of practice.

### DRUM CORPS

In the summer, drum corps is a daily diet of marching band. The instruments are strictly brass and percussion, and there are different age ranges and competition classes. Ages typically range from 10 to 21, and the number of corps members falls between 30 and 135. Tryouts generally happen in the fall. After the corps positions have been filled, practices to learn the routines begin.

Florida's 2002 Magic of Orlando had 126 corps members age 15 to 21 from Arizona, Alabama, Florida, Japan, Korea, North Carolina, and Massachusetts. Retiree David Stevenson of Florida, volunteer coordinator for the Magic of Orlando Drum Corps, is familiar with the 11-hour practice days, the nine-vehicle caravan that travels in the night, the eight-week 10,000-mile itinerary, school gym floor lodging, stopping at several city laundromats every 12 or 14 days, late night dinners, and cooking 320 hot dogs for 160 people. Stevenson says, "I just got hooked on drum corps—the music, the pageantry, the color, the excitement!"

Drum corps shows run 11.5 minutes and include three or four songs. They are judged on the same criteria as other marching bands. Show themes are diverse.

# The Rewards

**M**arching band offers many rewards. You may meet and become friends with many young people who enjoy the marching and the music as much as you do. Besides those friendships, you will grow better at whatever skill you shared with the band, and learn more about music and performing in front of a crowd.

Attending practices, learning the music and the drills, being on time, taking care of your equipment, working with teammates—all of these details require you to be responsible. If you can manage all those details and entertain people at the same time, then you will be a success and a credit to your band.

*The chance to perform in an exciting event like the Rose Parade is one of the benefits of being in a marching band.*

*Playing in a marching band teaches participants about leadership, cooperation, and responsibility.*

The teamwork you learn in marching band will pay off in life when you have to work with other people to achieve a goal. Learning how to do this at a young age is a very special lesson. As with many well-planned activities, marching band can be full of surprises. Whether it is a hail storm that interferes with a performance or a late bus that changes the day's plans, dealing with this large group activity will help you become flexible and able to deal with changes.

The skills you learn in band can be useful in your studies and life outside of school. In school, you will know more about how to manage your time and be organized. All the things you had to do in band—be on time, practice, work with the group—are things you have to do as a student, so you will already have good work skills.

Marching bands have followers. In the beginning, your friends and family will watch and listen to you. As your audience grows, more people will know about your band. If your band has been around for a while, it will have a reputation and a history. You will look forward to seeing familiar faces in certain cities and at annual competitions. You will be part of a family that loves music and marching, perfecting and performing. You might be the band that brought home a competition trophy or traveled to other states or countries.

The more you practice, the better you will be and the more opportunities will be offered to you. Whether you perform across the ocean or give a solo performance in a local parade, you will have lasting memories of marching and making music in the band. You will be able to close your eyes and hear the music and the clapping, feel the ground vibrating, and see flags waving and the audience smiling.

## UNUSUAL INSTRUMENTS

In addition to the regular marching band instruments, bands sometimes add a few special instruments like the mellophone, marching baritone, and frumpet. The mellophone looks like a trumpet but is keyed in F. It has trumpet fingering and a French horn mouthpiece. The marching baritone is like a regular baritone except the bell is at the front instead of facing up. A frumpet sounds like a trumpet and looks like a mellophone, but it is keyed in B flat and has the same fingering as a trumpet.

# Glossary

**alla breve** – A time signature with two or four half-notes in a bar.

**arpeggios** – The notes of a chord played one right after the other, either going up or going down.

**auxiliary** – Additional aspects of a marching band; this term usually refers to the band's color guard.

**battery** – A collection of similar instruments.

**block formation** – A grouping of the band in a square or rectangle.

**bottom stopper** – The ground end of the flag carried by a color guard.

**brass band** – A band made up of brass instruments such as French horns, trombones, trumpets, and tubas.

**cadence** – A marching step; when a marching band moves it develops a cadence that matches the time and tempo of the music.

**cascading effect** – A move that has the look of an orderly fall.

**charts** – Sheets of information that show where every band member should stand for different parts of their performance.

**close interval** – An alignment in which marching band squad members stand shoulder to shoulder or elbow to elbow.

**color guard** – An auxiliary part of the band that carries flags and adds visual interest to the band's routines.

**common time** – A rhythm pattern with two or four beats, often four quarter notes, in a measure.

**community band** – A band outside of school that gives instruction and opportunities to perform; this type of band is usually sponsored by a business or service group, and members often pay fees to belong.

**compound time** – A musical rhythm in which each beat in a bar is again divided into three smaller units with the value of a dotted note.

**counts** – Another term for beats of music.

**corps style** – A style of marching very similar to traditional military style but unique for its roll step type of marching.

**crescendo** – A gradual increase in the volume of a musical passage, also the peak of that passage.

**diagonal moves** – Parts of a marching band routine in which marchers make moves that are neither horizontal nor vertical.

**disburse** – To move out of a formation.

**dress** – A term that refers to how band members are spaced and lined up; dress is also used in commands indicating movement, such as dress right and dress left.

**drill** – An exercise; drill can also refer to the formations in a marching band show.

**drum corps** – A kind of marching band that uses brass and percussion instruments and focuses on field competition.

**drum major** – A student band leader who works closely with the band director and is able to lead the band on the field or in the parade.

**dynamics** – The volume of sound.

**finger** – To move one's hands to play an instrument

**flag bearer** – One who carries a flag.

**flank** – A 90 degree turn; flank moves make quarter turns.

**follow the leader** – A technique in which one person moves into formation and the rest follow.

**formations** – Visual effects created on a field by the bodies of marching band members.

**freeze** – A stop of movement not anticipated by the audience.

**harmonies** – Chords.

**hite or hut** – An extra syllable added to some voice commands to make them easier to hear and understand; a band may also answer commands by shouting hite or hut.

**licks** – Musical passages, or short series of notes that give a brief rhythmic formula; licks can also refer to special movements in marching.

**lineup** – The way the marchers stand next to each other.

**maneuvers** – Moves used by marching bands.

**mark time** – To march in place.

**measure** – The rhythm of a piece of music.

**oblique** – Term for a slanted move or 45-degree turn.

**phrasing** – The manner in which music has been divided for a performance.

**pipe band** – A type of marching band that uses bagpipes and other instruments.

**pitch** – The highness and lowness of a musical sound.

**pivot** – To turn.

**popping the knee** – Sticking the knee out during a marching maneuver.

**preseason** – Before the start of the regular program.

**rank and file** – Rows, or ranks, of marchers standing side by side and lines of marchers one behind the other.

**roll step** – A type of marching step that makes it look like one is gliding across the ground.

**routine** – A marching band performance that is made to match a piece of music.

**scales** – Arrangements of notes that go up or down in pitch.

**scout band** – Bands made up of Boy Scouts or Girl Scouts.

**scramble band** – University or college bands that use props, give funny shows, and move on the field in what looks like a disorganized way.

**sectional** – A part of the band with all the same kind of instruments, like a trombone sectional.

**show band** – A college band known for its high-stepping marching style.

**silk** – The flag that a color guard carries.

**stinger** – A sustained note that starts with a hard attack, backs off, and then crescendos.

**stride step** – Forward march or roll step.

**step off** – Term that means "starting to march."

**squad** – A marching band unit that moves together as a group.

**tab** – In color guard, the place where the bottom of the flag meets the pole.

**time signature** – Numbers behind the clef at the start of a piece of music that tell what rhythm the music should have; the top number tells the number of beats in each bar; the bottom number describes the beat as a part of a whole note.

**tone** – The music quality.

**tonguing attack** – A method of making sound on a wind instrument by using the tongue to direct the flow of air into the instrument.

**traditional marching band** – A military style band that uses woodwind, brass, and percussion instruments.

**up beat** – The last beat in a musical measure.

**whirl** – A complete turn.

# Internet Resources

**http://www.bands.org**
> Bands of America (BOA) hold events for more than 60,000 teens each year.

**http://www3.sk.sympatico/ca**
> The Canadian Band Association (CBA) supports school and community bands in Canada.

**http://www.dci.org**
> Drum Corps International (DCI) holds worldwide competitions for drum and bugle corps.

**http://website.lineone.net**
> The International Military Music Society (IMMS) has 1,300 members from 31 countries and supports youth brass, percussion, and pipe bands worldwide.

**http://www.nyb.ca**
> The National Youth Band of Canada recognizes music as a lifelong interest and gives young people musical opportunities.

**http://www.tob.org**
> Tournament of Bands (TOB) is a competitive band organization open to any middle school, high school, college, or university band.

**http://www.wgi.org**
> Winter Guard International (WGI) offers clinics on all color guard topics.

**http://www.wamsb.org**
> The World Association of Marching Show Bands (WAMSB) puts marching band competition on a world-class stage.

# Further Reading

Ardley, Neil. *Music, An Eyewitness Book.* New York: Dorling Kindersley Education, 1993.

Bailey, Wayne, and Thomas Caneva. *The Complete Marching Band Resource Manual.* Philadelphia: University of Pennsylvania Press, 1994.

Garty, Judy. *Marching Band Competition.* Broomall, Pennsylvania: Mason Crest Publishers, 2003.

Holston, Kim R. *The Marching Band Handbook.* Jefferson, North Carolina: McFarland and Company, 1994.

Koscielniak, Bruce. *The Story of the Incredible Orchestra.* Boston: Houghton Mifflin Co., 2000.

# Index

## PICTURE CREDITS

**Front and back cover:** Courtesy of the Pasadena Tournament of Roses/Rose Parade

Tim Jackson Photography: 2, 6, 15, 18, 21, 25, 28, 40, 46, 49; Courtesy of the Pasadena Tournament of Roses/Rose Parade: 38, 44, 50, 54; Courtesy of the Cal Band of the University of California at Berkeley: 8, 16, 33, 42, 56.

**JUDY GARTY** has been writing stories since she was in elementary school. A writer of news and magazine features for many years, she contributed to two regional Wisconsin history books and to *Chicken Soup for the Kid's Soul*. Her children's books include *Jeffrey Bezos*, a biography of the man who founded Amazon.com, and a second book for this series called *Marching Band Competition*. Sometimes Mrs. Garty teaches middle school, and she always enjoys cheering for a good marching band.